FLOODS

Chris Oxlade

WAYLAND

First published in 2007 by Wayland

Copyright © Wayland 2007

Wayland,
Hachette Children's Books
338 Euston Road,
London NW1 3BH

Wayland Australia
Level 17/207 Kent Street
Sydney, NSW 2000

Editor: Susie Brooks
Managing Editor: Rasha Elsaeed
Designer: Tim Mayer, MayerMedia
Picture Researcher: Kathy Lockley

British Library Cataloguing in Publication Data
Oxlade, Chris
  Floods. - (Natural Disasters)
  1. Floods - Juvenile literature
  I. Title
  551.4'89

ISBN 9780750249188

Wayland is a division of Hachette Children's Books, an
Hachette Livre UK company.

Photo credits: Cover, 1, 30, 31 ©Rafiqur Rahman/Reuters/
Corbis; Bckgd 2-48 ©Corbis; 4 ©Patrick Durand/Corbis;
6 ©Theo Allofs/Corbis; 7 ©Gabriel Mistral/Getty Images;
8 ©Reuters/Corbis; 9 ©Benjamin Lowy/Corbis; 10 ©Time &
Life Pictures, photo by Thomas D. Macavoy/Getty Images;
12 ©Getty Images (Hulton Archive); 13 ©Robert Rider/AP/PA
Photos; 14-15 ©Cees van Leeuwen; Cordaiy Photo Library/
Corbis; 16-17 ©Annie Griffith Belt/Corbis; 18 ©Alan Hawes/
Corbis Sygma; 19 ©Andrew Holbrooke/Corbis; 20-21
©Brooks Kraft/Corbis; 23, 24-25 ©Sankei Shimbun/Corbis
Sygma; 26 ©Kazuhiro Nogi/AFP/Getty Images; 27
©Hashimoto Noboru/Corbis Sygma; 29 ©Heldur Netocny/
Panos Pictures; 32-33 ©Utpal Baruah/Reuters/Corbis;
34 ©Marc Hill/Alamy Images; 36 ©Graeme Robertson/Getty
Images; 37, 38-39 ©Getty Images; 40-41 ©Bob
Sacha/Corbis; 42 ©Vincent Laforet/POOL/epa/Corbis; 43
©Lee Celano/ Reuters/Corbis; 44 ©Ed Pritchard/Getty
Images; 45 ©China News Photo/Reuters/Corbis

CONTENTS

What is a flood?

Since official records have been kept, floods have killed more people than all other natural disasters put together. A flood happens when water covers land that is normally dry. Most floods occur when rivers become so full that they overflow their banks, swamping the land alongside with water. Floods also happen on coasts, when the sea rises and flows across low-lying ground.

This flood in the streets of Ecouen, France was caused by a storm. Some higher areas remain dry, while on lower land the houses are submerged.

Flood hazards

The most deadly hazard of floods is deep or fast-flowing water, which can injure or drown people by trapping them underneath the surface. But floods bring many more hazards, too. Structures are damaged and even destroyed by fast-flowing water that breaks walls, weakens foundations and carries away light buildings. When buildings are submerged, flood water soaks into everything, ruining furnishings, fixtures, fittings and appliances. The water leaves a layer of smelly mud on everything it covers. Cars and other vehicles float away, even in quite shallow water.

Flood water also damages infrastructure, such as roads, railways, bridges, telephone and power lines, water supplies and sewers. The loss of water supplies is a major problem, as people forced to drink flood water are at risk from diseases such as cholera and dysentery. Floods also damage crops when they wash over fields.

The purple areas on this map show the parts of the world where floods happen most regularly. The blue lines show some of the world's major rivers.

Living with floods

Hundreds of millions of people live in flood-risk areas. These include tens of millions of residents of towns and cities who use rivers as a water supply and for transport. People farm the land alongside rivers because the water can be used for irrigating crops, and because floods bring mineral-rich sediments (soils) to the fields. People live on coasts to fish in the sea and because they enjoy the seaside environment. In crowded, less economically developed countries (LEDCs), land shortages often force poor people to live where floods occur.

CHINA'S SORROW

The three most deadly floods in recent history have happened on the same river – the Huang He (or Yellow River) in China. In 1931, between 1 million and 3.7 million people died in floods on the huge plains alongside the river. Up to 2 million died in 1887 and up to 1 million in 1938. The river is known as China's Sorrow.

River floods

Rivers drain water from the landscape and carry it to the sea. The area a river and its tributaries (smaller rivers that flow into it) drain is known as a drainage basin. A river tends to be steep near its source in hills or mountains, and almost level in its lower stages, nearer the coast. In the lower stages, a river has wide, flat floodplains alongside its channel. These plains are covered with water when the river floods.

The water cycle

Water flows down rivers because of the water cycle. This is the natural movement of water between the oceans, the atmosphere and the land. The Sun's heat makes water evaporate from the oceans, creating water vapour in the air. When this moist air moves over the land, some of the moisture condenses to form tiny water droplets that make up clouds. Rain then falls from the clouds onto the land and flows down rivers back to the sea.

MEASURING FLOODS

Hydrologists (scientists who study rivers) describe the severity of a flood by how often such a flood is likely to happen. The more severe a flood, the less likely it is to occur. For example, a five-year flood is a flood that has a one in five chance of happening in a year. It is not very severe. A hundred-year flood is much more severe. It has only a one in a hundred chance of happening each year.

You can see the wide, flat floodplains stretching etiher side of this winding river in Western Australia.

Where flood water comes from

Rain either soaks into the ground or runs off into streams and rivers. Floods normally happen after long periods of rain, when the ground becomes so saturated (soaked) that water has to run off the surface. During heavy rain, the level of water in a river gradually rises. If more water flows into the river than can fit into its channel, the river overflows its banks. As the water moves down the river, so does the flooding. There may be flooding hundreds of kilometres from where rain fell. Flood water also comes from snow that melts quickly.

River flood patterns

Flooded streets are a regular problem for residents when monsoon rains hit the islands of the Philippines.

Rivers normally flood at particular times of year. This pattern of flooding depends on the climate in the drainage basin. In some places, rainfall is highest in winter, so floods are most likely then. In other places, summer floods are more common. Spring floods happen when rivers fill with melting snow as the weather warms up after winter.

Monsoons

The monsoon is a wind that blows in southern Asia. Monsoon floods happen during a period called the summer monsoon, when cool, moist air from over the Indian Ocean drops heavy rain on the land. Many rivers in southern Asia flood annually during the summer monsoon.

7

Flash floods and coastal floods

A flash flood is a damaging rush of water that arrives suddenly, often without warning. Flash floods are caused by unusually heavy rain, which can turn a stream into a deadly torrent. Flash floods last only briefly, but they can be very destructive. Coastal floods happen along low-lying coasts when the sea level rises and water flows inland. Coastal floods are caused by high tides, storms and tsunami waves.

Flash floods

Extremely heavy rain is needed to produce a flash flood. The rain normally comes from severe thunderstorms that are slow moving, so drop all their rain in one place. The rain falls so quickly that the ground cannot soak it up, and most of it runs off the surface. Flash floods can strike at any time of year. They normally happen in hilly areas, where the water pours down steep slopes into river valleys.

The deep, fast-flowing water of a flash flood is dangerous to wade through. This fireman was part of a rescue operation after violent storms hit Sommière, France in 2002.

Flash floods have all the dangers of river floods and more. They can arrive so suddenly that people and cars are washed away. The fast-moving water picks up debris such as logs and boulders, and these batter everything in their path. The force of the water can even push over buildings and rip up roads.

Low-lying coasts

There are many coasts around the world where the land is just a few metres above sea level. These coastal plains are always at risk from flooding. In places such as the Netherlands, some land is actually lower than sea level.

TSUNAMI SPEEDS AND HEIGHTS

In deep oceans, tsunami waves (see text below) can travel at nearly 1,000 kph, but may be only a metre high. When the waves reach shallower water, they slow down but grow in height. Tsunami waves 30 metres high have been recorded hitting the coast of Japan.

Thousands of buildings, such as these in Banda Aceh, Indonesia, were completely destroyed by a devastating tsunami that hit many Asian coastlines in December 2004.

Tides and surges

Tides happen because the gravity of the Moon and Sun attracts the water in the Earth's oceans. This attraction makes the surface of the oceans bulge upwards slightly. When the forces of gravity of the Moon and Sun pull in the same direction, the tide can rise high enough to flood the coast.

Severe storms, such as hurricanes, are made up of areas of low air pressure. The low pressure allows the sea surface to rise upwards slightly. The high winds in storms also push the water before them. Together, the low pressure and strong winds build up a mound of water several metres high, known as a storm surge. The worst flooding happens where a storm surge combines with high waves and a high tide.

Tsunamis

A tsunami is a series of waves, usually set off by an earthquake but also by landslides or volcanic eruptions. The waves travel across the ocean until they hit a coast, when they rear up and surge inland, smashing everything in their path and causing severe flooding.

NORTH SEA COASTS, 1953

The night of 31 January 1953 saw one of the most violent storms of the twentieth century hit the North Sea. The surge of water pushed up by the storm, combined with a high tide and powerful waves, broke through sea defences and caused severe flooding on the low-lying coasts of the Netherlands and England. More than 2,000 people died. It was one of the worst natural disasters to occur in Europe in modern times.

The district of Zeeland in the southern Netherlands was overwhelmed by the floods of 1953.

Low-lying landscape

The North Sea lies between the northern European mainland and the British Isles. On the sides of its narrow, southern section, the coastal plains are only a few metres above the sea. In many places they are actually below sea level. There are also many low-lying islands along the coasts, and river estuaries snake far inland. In the south-west of the Netherlands, the land is made up of the deltas of the Rhine and Meuse rivers, which include many islands. A delta is an area formed from sediment that is deposited by rivers as they near the sea.

The people who settled in these areas began building coastal defences more than a thousand years ago, as flooding was always a threat to them. There is now an extensive system of dykes (flood walls) protecting the land. One-fifth of the Netherlands is land that people have reclaimed from the sea by building dykes and pumping out water. These sections of land are called polders. The ground in them is often several metres below sea level. Some areas of eastern England are similarly formed, and the coast here is also protected by dykes and sea walls.

Hurricane-strength winds

The storm that caused the 1953 floods was an Atlantic low-pressure system. Its centre moved around the north of Scotland, eastwards across the North Sea and into the Netherlands. The low pressure and hurricane-force winds of more than 117 kph pushed a mound of water, or storm surge, down the North Sea ahead of them.

Unfortunately, the storm surge arrived together with an unusually high tide. Along the coast of the Netherlands the sea level rose up to 3.36 metres above normal, and along the English coast it rose up to 2.97 metres above normal. On top of this, huge waves pounded the shore. Sea defences failed under the immense pressure, and sea water poured inland.

DISASTER DAYS

30 JANUARY 1953
Powerful eastbound Atlantic weather system moves into the North Sea.

31 JANUARY
4 pm Flooding begins in Lincolnshire, England.

1 FEBRUARY
1 am Canvey Island in England is flooded when its sea walls collapse.

3 am First dykes collapse in the Netherlands.

3.24 am Water levels peak in the Netherlands.

5.30 am Major dyke, the Groenendijk, collapses in the Netherlands.

2 FEBRUARY
Major rescue effort begins in the Netherlands; two days later the Delta Committee is formed to instigate repairs and restoration of dykes.

NOVEMBER 1953
Repairs are finally completed to the Netherlands' broken dykes.

MAY 1958
Delta Law is passed for construction of the Delta Works (see page 15).

MAY 1984
Thames Flood Barrier is officially opened in the UK.

FLOOD COSTS

- 1,835 deaths in the Netherlands
- 307 deaths in England
- 25 deaths in Belgium
- 46,000 homes destroyed in the Netherlands
- 24,000 homes destroyed in England

Debris floats around the Dutch town of Stellendam during the floods of 1953.

No warnings

The people in danger areas on both sides of the North Sea had little or no warning of the coming floods. At the time, there were no weather satellites or forecasting computers. Weather forecasters knew that the storm was on the way, but they could not predict its track or the height of the storm surge. By the time people realized how severe the flooding would be, it was too late. In the 1950s there were no radio stations broadcasting at night when warnings were needed. There was not enough time to raise the alarm by telephone, by telegraph, or by word of mouth. In the Netherlands, the telephone lines had been brought down by the storm.

Dyke failures

In the Netherlands, a programme of dyke improvements had been underway for many years, but had been interrupted by the Second World War. Money had been spent on repairing bombed dykes, and on building new polders, but many old dykes were still in a poor state. As the water rose, some of the dykes collapsed. Others held but the water flowed over their tops. In all, 89 dykes failed, allowing water to flood 2,000 square kilometres of polders.

The water reached up to 60 kilometres inland and lay 10 metres deep in some polders. Communities were completely submerged, and houses were washed away by the rush of water. The surge also pushed water up rivers and inland. Parts of the city of Rotterdam were flooded as water filled the docks and overflowed into the streets.

The streets of Canvey Island, in the Thames estuary in south-east England, were left completely under water after flood defences failed.

SHIP BLOCKS DYKE

In the early morning of 1 February, a section of dyke north of the Dutch city of Rotterdam, called the Groenendijk, collapsed, allowing water surging up the Hollandse IJssel River to escape. This threatened millions of people. The captain of a ship called *de Twee Gebroeders* (*The Two Brothers*) was asked to manoeuvre his ship into the breach (gap). He succeeded, and the flow was blocked. His action probably saved thousands of lives.

Continued chaos

In England, there was flooding over 1,000 square kilometres of Lincolnshire, Norfolk, Suffolk and Essex. Coastal towns and farmland were flooded as dykes and sea walls collapsed. Canvey Island, in the Thames estuary, was swamped with water. The storm surge travelled up the Thames and flooded the district of West Ham in East London.

Most victims were woken from their sleep by the roaring flood water. They climbed on to roofs, clung to the wreckage of their homes, or were swept away in the water. The floods began to retreat the next morning, but at the next high tide water came through the broken Dutch dykes, destroyed more houses and claimed more lives.

Rescue efforts

In the Netherlands, the telephone network was lost and roads were submerged, making communications impossible. People were unable to report the situation to the authorities, so at first the extent and severity of the flooding was not known and people had to fend for themselves. Villagers used boats to rescue people from the water or trapped on roofs, and moved them to higher ground. Amateur radio operators moved in to help broadcast information. Eventually, a large-scale rescue operation began on 2 February. International help included the assistance of US army helicopters and French army engineers. Over the next few days, 72,000 people were evacuated from flooded homes and supplies such as food, clothes and furniture arrived by air. The situation was similar in England, with 30,000 evacuated.

Making repairs

The sea defences in the Netherlands and England were repaired over the next few months. There were problems with this in the Netherlands as water continued to flow into the polders even after the sea level had returned to normal. Large concrete blocks called caissons had to be dropped into the breaches in the dykes, as other materials were simply washed away. Repairs were not fully completed until November.

EYEWITNESS

All of a sudden we heard what sounded like a big explosion. We looked over by the railway line and we could see like a big wave come over the top and that's when it caught all the prefabs [temporary houses]. And seconds after that, and I can still hear it today if I close my eyes, I can hear the people screaming 'Help us!' because the poor people couldn't get out.

Derek Swann, Felixstowe, England

Long-term answers

The 1953 flood forced the governments in the Netherlands and the UK to plan new flood-defence programmes. In the Netherlands, the Delta Works (*Deltawerken*) was started. This consists of a series of giant barriers across the estuaries in the south-west. Some are dams and some are barriers with gates that close when storm surges threaten. The barriers allow ships to pass, and also allow salt water to enter the estuaries so that the natural saltwater environment is maintained. The scheme was finally completed in 1998. In England, sea defences on the east coast were strengthened, and the Thames Barrier was built to protect low-lying areas of London from future storm surges. Today, weather forecasting and storm tracking are far better than they were in 1953, and each country has a good storm warning system.

Could it happen again?

Although the combination of storm and high tide that caused the 1953 floods was unlikely, it could happen again. New sea defences should hold back the water, and flood warnings should warn people to evacuate in plenty of time. However, in this area the land is slowly sinking because of movements in the Earth's crust, and the sea is gradually rising because of global warming. Sea defences on both sides of the North Sea will have to be continuously upgraded in the future.

HIGH-RISK REGION

The areas of the Netherlands and England flooded in 1953 have a record of major floods. In both 1099 and 1421, more than 100,000 people were killed by floods in England and the Netherlands.

This photo shows a section of the Oosterschelde, one of the main barriers that now protect the Netherlands from coastal floods.

MISSISSIPPI RIVER, USA, 1993

The Mississippi is one of the world's major rivers. Its water is vital for hundreds of communities along its banks, and it is the USA's busiest waterway. But when the Mississippi floods, the results are catastrophic. One of the worst floods on the Mississippi happened in 1993, when record rainfall fell in the Midwest (a region between the Ohio River and the Rocky Mountains). Known as the Great Flood of '93, it was one of the USA's most costly natural disasters.

The Mississippi River

The Mississippi runs for 3,766 kilometres and is the USA's second longest river. It flows from north to south through the centre of the USA and empties into the Gulf of Mexico. Here, sediment carried downstream forms a wide delta. The Mississippi has several large tributaries, including the Missouri (the longest river in the USA) and the Ohio. The area drained by the Mississippi and its tributaries is the third largest drainage basin in the world, covering 3,230,490 square kilometres – 41 per cent of the area of the USA. On average, the Mississippi drains 18,100 cubic metres of water into the Gulf of Mexico every second.

The flow level of the Mississippi rises and falls during the year. The highest flows normally happen in spring and early summer, when water from summer rains combines with water from melting snow in the Rocky Mountains. This raises the water level in the middle section of the river and is the time when floods are most likely.

River development

Development along the Mississippi and its tributaries began in the eighteenth century, as settlers explored along the rivers and founded new settlements. The river became important for transport and trade, and gradually the floodplains were turned to farmland. Towns and cities grew up alongside the river. The Mississippi is now a major resource that supplies water for cities, industries and farms along its banks. It also carries 420 million tonnes per year of cargo such as crops, coal, steel and aluminium and chemicals. The river is navigable (sailable) from Minnesota in the north to the Gulf of Mexico in the south. However, the river that people rely on is also a great danger to them. It has flooded dozens of times in the past, swamping the towns, cities and farms on the floodplains with water.

Cargo and passenger boats navigate the busy Mississippi River through St Louis. This city escaped from flooding in 1993.

Previous protection

Flood protection schemes were built along the Mississippi after a disastrous flood in 1927. There are now thousands of kilometres of levees (protecting walls) along the middle and lower sections of the river that keep flood water in the river channel. Dozens of dams on the Missouri, Ohio and Tennessee rivers prevent flood water from flowing into the Mississippi. The river has also been dredged (cleared of sediment) and straightened to allow its water to flow more swiftly to the sea.

Local people in the Midwest build up a levee with sand sacks, to try to keep the flood waters back.

Record rainfall

The Midwest normally experiences summer storms when cool, dry air from the north meets warm, moist air from the south. Usually the storms move away eastwards, but in 1993 a weather system over the Atlantic blocked them in and they stayed over land from April to July. In the states of Illinois, Iowa, Minnesota, North Dakota and South Dakota it was the wettest summer on record, with up to three times the normal rainfall. Water hit record levels along the lower Missouri, Des Moines River and the middle part of the Mississippi. In many places the levees were not high enough, and water poured over them on to the floodplains. Forecasters knew the floods were on the way, but they could not have predicted that the rains would be so heavy or last for so long.

In many places flooding reached rooftop level, submerging homes completely. Entire streets, such as this one in West Alton, Missouri, disappeared under the murky water.

Flood damage

The water poured into riverside towns and villages. Tens of thousands of people had to leave their homes for temporary accommodation on higher ground. Most of those affected were poorer people who could afford only to live in the cheaper, flood-risk areas. Those that stayed found electricity and water supplies cut off for weeks after power and water supply plants were drowned. The flood water washed sewage out of the drains into the streets. Thousands of farms were submerged. The water washed away millions of tonnes of precious topsoil and ruined crops by leaving them covered in sediment. Main highways, railways and airports were flooded, and river bridges were closed in case they collapsed. Barge movements on the Mississippi were stopped for two months because of the strong currents. The flood lasted from May to September. Some places remained under water for nearly 200 days.

EYEWITNESS

❝ I think it's going to take a miracle this time. We talked about leaving after the 1973 flood, and I think we'll leave after this one. We're too old to fight it any more. ❞

Ginnie Eller, Grafton, Illinois

After the flood

As the waters of the Great Flood of '93 slowly retreated, people could finally return home to inspect the destruction. Residents pulled water-damaged belongings, furniture and carpets out into the streets, and tried to wash away the stinking mud that had been deposited by the water. Those without flood insurance were given flood-relief assistance by the government to help make repairs and replace belongings. For some people, the thought of returning to a place that could flood again was too much. They abandoned their homes and moved away. In a few places, whole communities were abandoned. The government offered to buy flooded properties so that people could afford to move. About 7,500 households took up the offer.

EYEWITNESS

❝ This part of the country has never seen such heavy rainfall and never experienced such heavy flooding. The magnitude [size] and duration of flooding were almost overwhelming and it's a tribute to people that they continued to battle to save their homes, farms and communities. ❞

Kenneth D. King, head of the regional headquarters of the National Weather Service in Kansas City

After the floods had retreated, people worked hard to recover their belongings. The dirty water damaged nearly everything in this house.

FLOOD COSTS

- 50 deaths
- 54,000 people evacuated
- 50,000 homes damaged or destroyed
- 75 towns completely flooded
- 80,000 square kilometres of land covered
- Overall cost of damage: US$20 billion

Rebuilding levees

Once water levels had returned to normal, work began on repairing the breached levees. The flood started a debate about the actual usefulness of levees. Generally they work well, keeping hundreds of towns and thousands of farms safe from regular flooding. But some scientists argue that stopping flood water from spreading over the floodplain is a bad thing as it forces the water to move downstream, where it does more damage in places where there are no levees. However, for the time being levees will remain the main flood protection on the Mississippi. They cannot be removed because they would leave millions of people at the mercy of seasonal high waters.

Floodplain development

The Mississippi's floodplain is a vulnerable place to live and work. There is always a risk of this land being submerged in the natural process of flooding. However, new commercial and residential developments have been built on the Mississippi's floodplain in the years since the Great Flood, some on land flooded in 1993. Levees have been heightened to give extra protection to the land.

Building developers argue that the risk of flooding is small. Meanwhile critics claim that the land is bound to flood at some time in the future, and that covering the floodplain with concrete and asphalt will make flooding worse by forcing more water into places downstream. Building on the floodplain also destroys wetlands along the river's banks – these swampy areas naturally store water during floods, making flooding elsewhere less severe.

JAPANESE TSUNAMI, 1993

The country of Japan is a curved chain of islands that lie in the Pacific Ocean. Movements in the Earth's crust mean the islands are rocked by many earthquakes every year. These earthquakes regularly cause tsunamis that wash over the land. On 12 July 1993, a tsunami struck the coast of the Japanese island of Hokkaido. Worse hit was a small island close to Hokkaido, called Okushiri. In all, 239 people died as the waves caused devastating floods.

THE RICHTER SCALE

The Richter scale gives a measure of the power of an earthquake. Seismologists (scientists who study earthquakes) rate earthquake tremors between 1 and 10, with higher numbers being the more powerful. An increase of 1 on the scale (say from 6 to 7) means an increase of 10 times the power.

Shaking the sea

It was late evening on 12 July when an earthquake measuring 7.7 on the Richter scale happened deep under the Sea of Japan, about 30 kilometres west of Hokkaido. The jolting movement of the seabed made the water rise and fall, which set off a terrifying tsunami. The fast-moving waves spread in all directions. They hit Okushiri less than four minutes later. As they approached the island, they gained height and were between 5 and 10 metres tall when they struck the shore. The waves bent around the island so that they attacked every coast, not just the west coast that faces the Sea of Japan. Tsunami waves also hit the coast of Hokkaido, and the shores of Russia and Korea which are located west of the Sea of Japan.

Island risk

The island of Okushiri has a population of about 5,300 people. Its towns and villages are located mainly around the coast, where people work in the fishing and tourism industries. This means that most of Okushiri's residents live near the sea, where their homes are at risk from tsunamis.

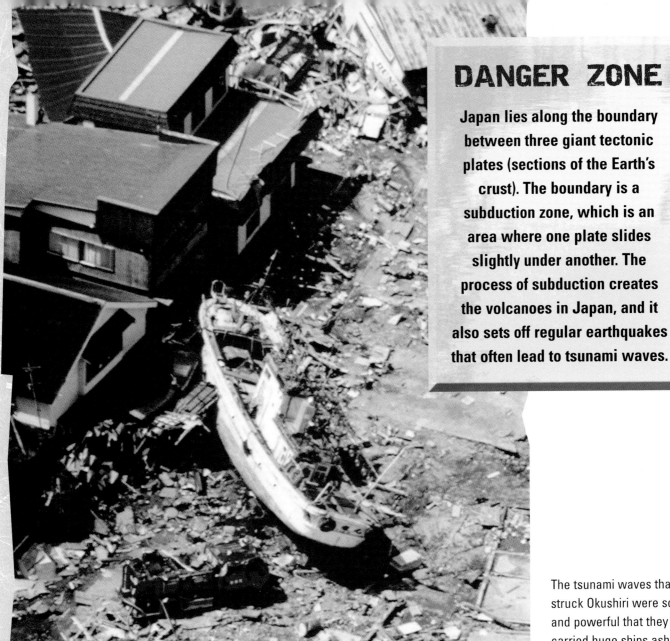

Japan lies along the boundary between three giant tectonic plates (sections of the Earth's crust). The boundary is a subduction zone, which is an area where one plate slides slightly under another. The process of subduction creates the volcanoes in Japan, and it also sets off regular earthquakes that often lead to tsunami waves.

The tsunami waves that struck Okushiri were so big and powerful that they carried huge ships ashore. This fishing boat lies among the debris of buildings left behind when the water subsided.

Towering waves

When the waves hit Okushiri, they broke and washed ashore. They were most powerful in the south and west of the island, where the water reached between 10 and 20 metres above sea level. In one small valley on the south-west coast, the waves sloshed a staggering 31 metres up the valley sides. Water washed right over the peninsula at the southern end of Okushiri, creating floods up to 20 metres deep.

FLOOD COSTS

- 239 deaths
- 540 houses destroyed
- 1,980 houses damaged
- 31 public buildings damaged
- Total cost: about US$78 million

Effects of the tsunami

Parts of Okushiri Island were protected by concrete sea walls up to 4.5 metres high, designed to deflect the power of tsunami waves. However, on 12 July 1993, the powerful waves broke through them. The waves smashed into coastal towns and villages. They hit buildings, cars and trucks, fishing boats and other objects, smashing them into pieces. The debris was swept along in the water, acting as a battering ram that destroyed more property. Houses, schools, factories, bridges, roads, railways, power plants and water works were damaged.

The first wave filled the village of Aonae, on the southern peninsula of Okushiri, with several metres of water. It was soon followed by a second, larger wave, which hurled fishing boats from the harbour into the streets. The waves that hit the west coast of Hokkaido caused extensive damage to several towns. The damage from the tsunami came on top of damage to buildings caused by the earthquake and also by landslides set off by the tremors.

Fire hazards

In several places, as buildings were knocked down, gas pipes shattered and gas canisters and tanks of heating oil were tipped over. Electrical installations created sparks that lit these fuels, and the resulting fires burned out of control through buildings that had survived the waves. In Aonae, fire destroyed 340 homes. Debris, washed over the island's roads, made it impossible for fire engines to tackle the fires efficiently.

Fires burned much of the fishing village of Aonae to ashes after the tsunami struck.

Lucky escapes

The waves hit in the late evening, when most people were indoors. In all 239 people were killed, most of them trapped in their homes or washed away by the water. The death toll may well have been higher, but Japanese people know that tsunamis can be set off by earthquakes, and many ran or cycled to high ground as soon as they felt the earthquake's tremors.

The Japan Meteorological Agency had detected the earthquake and issued a tsunami warning less than five minutes later. But by then waves were already arriving on the shores of Okushiri and Hokkaido. On coasts further from the earthquake, the warnings allowed people to get clear.

WARNING!

Japan was not the only country on tsunami alert. The Russian Tsunami Warning Centre issued a warning 20 minutes after the earthquake, and Korean authorities raised the alarm after 33 minutes. The Pacific Tsunami Warning Centre issued warnings for the whole north-west Pacific area.

Lessons learned

Since the 1993 disaster, a completely new tsunami protection system has been constructed on Okushiri. There are a total of 14 kilometres of new sea walls, ranging in height from 5.4-11.7 metres, designed to stop tsunamis from running up into villages. Sets of floodgates have been built where the island's main rivers reach the sea. When a tsunami warning is sounded, the gates close to stop waves moving up the river and spreading inland.

In Aonae, the village worst affected by the 1993 flood, an evacuation area was built on stilts, nearly 7 metres above the ground. This gives people a safe place to escape to if a tsunami approaches. There are also 40 well-signposted evacuation routes leading from the coastal villages to higher ground.

All the houses on the island now have special radio receivers that are tuned in to broadcast tsunami warnings. All residents have been given disaster prevention handbooks that give advice about what to do in the event of another tsunami.

The victims of the Okushiri disaster faced the prospect of having to completely rebuild their lives. New safety measures aim to protect people from this kind of suffering in future.

Evacuation drills are regular practice in many parts of Japan, to make sure people are prepared for the event of a future earthquake or tsunami.

Better warnings

Japan has a sophisticated tsunami warning system, operated by the Japan Meteorological Agency (JMA). The system was good in 1993, but has been improved further. It can now issue warnings within three minutes of an earthquake. At the Japan Meteorological Agency, the computerized Earthquake and Tsunami Observation System (ETOS) continuously receives data from 180 seismic sensors across Japan and 80 water-level sensors at sea. This information helps scientists to predict where tsunamis might strike. The JMA has direct links to broadcasting organizations, and tsunami warnings appear automatically on television screens and radio stations. There are also satellite links to local authorities, who operate sirens and loudspeaker systems to tell people to evacuate.

THE GREAT SANRIKU TSUNAMI

One of the worst tsunamis to hit Japan was the Great Sanriku Tsunami, which happened on 15 June 1896. It was set off by an extremely powerful earthquake measuring 8.5 on the Richter scale. The waves damaged 275 kilometres of coastline in the north-east of Honshu Island, leaving 28,000 people dead.

Information for the future

Scientists collected a great deal of data about the 1993 tsunami. They measured how far the waves had reached inland, investigated why sea defences had collapsed, looked at the damage caused, how people reacted, how the emergency services responded, and how the road network and telephone networks were affected. This information helped them to design new tsunami defences and disaster plans.

No matter how good warning systems and protection schemes become, the coast of Japan will always be a potentially dangerous place to live. Tsunamis like the one that struck Okushiri in 1993 can arrive within minutes of an earthquake, allowing no time for escape.

INDIA AND BANGLADESH, 2004

Bangladesh and the north-east of India are two parts of the world that suffer regular floods. Huge rivers overflow here nearly every summer because of monsoon rains. The year 2004 brought the worst floods for many decades to Bangladesh and India. Millions of people were affected. Most people who live here are poor farmers, and floods have a greater effect on them than they do on people in more economically developed countries (MEDCs).

Three great rivers

The landscape of north-east India and Bangladesh is dominated by three major rivers. The Ganges (known as the Padma in Bangladesh) flows in from the west, through the state of Bihar. The Brahmaputra (known as the Jamuna in Bangladesh) flows in from the east, through the state of Assam. Both of these rivers drain water from the great mountain range of the Himalayas. They meet in Bangladesh, where they are joined by another major river, the Meghna.

RIVERSIDE LIVING

Northern India and Bangladesh are highly populated places. Tens of millions of people live and farm on the floodplains of the three rivers. The rivers are vital resources. They bring water and silt that help crops to grow, and are also important transport routes. However, they can bring catastrophic floods, putting millions of lives at risk.

Delta and floodplains

In the south of Bangladesh, the rivers break up into many channels that flow across the Ganges delta and into the Bay of Bengal. The Ganges delta is the world's largest delta, and was formed by the sediment washed along by the rivers. There are wide floodplains along all these rivers. In fact, two-thirds of Bangladesh is made up of floodplains.

Monsoon season

Like most floods in northern India and Bangladesh, the floods of 2004 were caused by heavy monsoon rains. The monsoon season in this area lasts from mid-May until October. It occurs when heat builds up over the land as the sunshine becomes stronger in April. The warm air rises, forming an area of low pressure. As this happens, cool, moist air is drawn towards the land from over the Indian Ocean. This causes heavy rain when it crosses the land and rises upwards over the Himalayas.

Most people living in this region farm small areas of land, growing crops such as rice, jute and tea for themselves. These farmers are preparing a paddy field for rice planting on the huge floodplains of Madhupur, Bangladesh.

RECORD RAINS

The region of northern India and Bangladesh is one of wettest parts of the world. In some places, a massive 2.5 metres of rain can fall in a single month during the monsoon season.

The 2004 flood

The floods in 2004 affected the north Indian states of Assam and Bihar, and much of Bangladesh. The floods began in early July as water from the Himalayas filled the Ganges and Brahmaputra rivers, making them flow over flood-protection embankments. In many places the water was over head height, and fast flowing. In Bangladesh, flooding was worst where the two rivers meet. The capital, Dhaka, was badly affected. The flood water drained slowly south through Bangladesh, and the floods subsided by the middle of August. Some places were submerged for three or four weeks.

In many areas the flood waters were trapped on the wrong side of anti-flood embankments, leaving pools of stagnant water. In September, just as the situation appeared to be improving, more rain fell. This was the heaviest rain in 50 years, and it caused further serious flooding in Bangladesh, affecting places that had escaped the first onslaught.

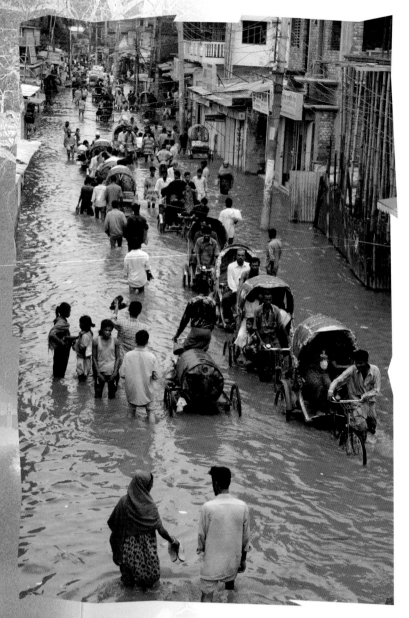

In some streets, flood water levels were low enough for people to wade through. Elsewhere, flooding was dangerously deep.

CYCLONE FLOODING

Bangladesh suffers river floods nearly every year. But every few years much more dangerous floods arrive from the sea. Cyclones (hurricane-strength storms) move up through the Bay of Bengal and hit the Ganges delta. The land here is only a metre or two above sea level, and flood surges and waves can drown coasts and islands. In 1991, a cyclone here killed 140,000 people.

❝ We tried to stay in our home, but it was too dangerous and we had to go to the relief shelter. People helped each other with food but our house was destroyed, apart from the roof and one wall. We have moved back and patched up the walls with paper. ❞

Helena Chaudhury, Velanagar, Bangladesh

The flood waters swept through thousands of villages, destroying millions of homes built from jute and bamboo. Tens of millions of people were in danger, including 36 million Bangladeshis – a quarter of the population. Many affected areas had not been flooded for decades, and people were unprepared. They had the choice of escaping to higher ground or staying in their flooded homes, where they were at risk of drowning, catching diseases and going hungry. Many were trapped on roofs, in trees and on patches of high ground, surrounded by water. Snakes were a danger as they tried to find dry land, too. More than a thousand people drowned in the deep flood water. Crops that were growing in the fields were ruined, and stores of grain from previous harvests became soaked. Roads, railways and telecommunications systems were all damaged.

Some buildings collapsed completely in the floods. This house in Dhaka, Bangladesh, fell on its side.

Rescue and recovery

The wide area of India and Bangladesh covered by the 2004 floods, and the millions of people involved, meant that evacuating everybody was impossible. Some people were rescued from roofs, trees and islands by boat and taken to safer ground. The governments of India and Bangladesh, together with national and international aid agencies, set up emergency shelters and distributed food by helicopter. Unfortunately there was not enough food to go round, and in some places people fought over it.

As the flood waters subsided, the authorities assessed what the people affected would need in the short term and the long term. The main needs were clean water supplies, sanitation, food and shelter.

MAKING IT WORSE

The Himalayan mountains run east from northern India through neighbouring Nepal and Bhutan. About 60 per cent of Nepal's forests have been cut down, and the bare ground left allows monsoon rains to flow quickly down into the Ganges, making floods worse than before. Floods are also made worse when water is released from dams in Nepal, Bhutan and India to prevent local water levels from becoming too high.

The Indian Air Force throw emergency food supplies to stranded flood victims in the state of Assam, India.

FLOOD COSTS

- **More than 1,000 deaths**
- **8.5 million homes destroyed**
- **35 million people affected**
- **Millions put at risk from disease**
- **Two-thirds of Bangladesh flooded**
- **Total cost of damage: about US$3 billion**

Immediate problems

The threat of water-borne diseases such as cholera and dysentery was severe, as millions of people had no fresh water and had to drink from the muddy floods. Governments and aid agencies set up water supplies and sanitation systems, and distributed water purification tablets and clean water containers. Despite their efforts, thousands of people were admitted to clinics and dozens died from disease.

The next problem was the lack of food because of the loss of crops and grain stores. Food rations were supplied, including high-energy biscuits for children. People returned to their homes to try to make repairs, rescue their crops and start farming again. Millions of people, already poor, were left worse off than they were before the flood.

Future floods

Floods are a fact of life for the people of northern India and Bangladesh. Major floods will always happen, but things can be done to make the effects less damaging. For example, in Bangladesh money is being invested in flood shelters and rescue boats. Flood protection schemes, on the other hand, may not be the answer. In fact, at the moment they make floods worse. Embankments along rivers, built to stop rivers overflowing, actually stop flood water from draining away and therefore prolong floods. In India, dams and barriers are poorly maintained and often make floods worse when they happen. Some experts suggest that all flood barriers should be removed, allowing flood waters to spread across the whole floodplain. This would allow the floods to pass more quickly.

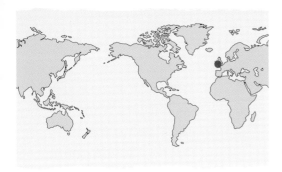

BOSCASTLE VALLEY, UK, 2004

The village of Boscastle is on the north coast of Cornwall, a county in the south-west of the UK. Boscastle's economy relies mainly on tourists, who come to see its traditional buildings and the tiny natural harbour. On 16 August 2004, at the height of the tourist season, extremely heavy rainfall struck the hills inland from Boscastle. Water swept down the valley into the village, causing one the UK's most damaging floods. In a few minutes, many of the residents' livelihoods were ruined.

The village of Boscastle lies in a valley leading down to the sea. Some of the flood damage is visible in this photograph.

Boscastle's valley

Boscastle is situated in a narrow, steep-sided, wooded valley. Part of the village stretches up one side of the valley, and part lies in the valley bottom. Boscastle's harbour is the only natural harbour in the area. The village was a busy port in the nineteenth century, but its importance declined by the beginning of the twentieth century, when railways took over freight transport.

The Valency River flows through Boscastle's valley. It is a small river, just a few metres wide, which runs through the village, through the harbour and into the sea. It is joined in the middle of the village by another river, the Jordan, which flows down through the upper part of Boscastle. The Boscastle coast is quite rugged. The land rises steeply from the village to moorland a few kilometres inland, which is more than 300 metres above sea level. The Valency and Jordan rivers flow down from these moors. The source of the Valency is just a few kilometres inland from the village. The drainage basins of both rivers added together total only 20 square kilometres.

Flood rains

The Boscastle flood was caused by an unusual set of weather conditions. That day, there was a sea breeze that drew in very damp air from over the sea. This air met dry, cool air blowing from over the land. The two airflows mixed and were forced upwards, forming a line of towering thunderstorms along the coast. The storms began dropping torrential rain at about midday. They were very slow moving, and in some places extremely heavy rain fell for several hours. On the moors above Boscastle, about 12 centimetres of rain fell in the afternoon. The ground was already saturated from earlier rains, and the water ran off the land into the river valleys.

DISASTER DAYS

16 AUGUST 2004
12 pm Torrential rain begins to fall over Cornwall.

1 pm Water level in the Valency River begins to rise.

3.30 pm Valency overflows its banks in Boscastle.

3.45 pm Cars begin to float in the Boscastle tourist car park.

4.10 pm First cars are washed down through the village.

4.30 pm Access roads to the village are closed.

4.45 pm First rescue helicopters arrive on the scene.

5 pm Flood waters approach peak level; visitor centre collapses.

6 pm Flood levels begin to subside.

17 AUGUST 2004
Search-and-rescue operation continues; divers check the harbour.

18 AUGUST 2004
Residents are escorted back to gather belongings before restoration work begins.

APRIL 2005
New storm drain is completed in Boscastle.

MAY 2005
Villagers celebrate the regeneration of Boscastle and launch a new tourist season.

No flood warning

Experts at the UK's Environment Agency knew that flooding was a possibility in Boscastle, and they had a flood-risk map showing which areas of the village were in danger. The agency takes information from weather forecasters and from water-level monitors on the rivers to try to predict floods. Very heavy rain was forecast for the area in August 2004, but nobody knew exactly where it would fall. In fact, in places just a few kilometres away from Boscastle, there was almost no rain at all. Because the rain was so localized, the flood was not predicted and no warning was issued.

These cars, swept along and wrecked by the flood water, were left buried in mud after the flooding subsided.

FREAK FLOWS

It is estimated that at the peak of the flood 180 cubic metres of water poured through Boscastle every second, and that before the flood subsided about 2 million tonnes of water flowed through the village.

Emergency teams had to rescue some residents from rooftops. This screen grab shows a girl being winched to safety by an RAF helicopter crew.

The sudden flood

The valleys of the Valency and the Jordan acted like giant funnels, channelling the water down to Boscastle. In the mid-afternoon, the Valency burst its banks. The flood water continued to rise, reaching its maximum depth at about 5 pm, when it was 3 metres deep in the streets. The water built up behind walls, bridges and temporary dams made of debris. As these collapsed, surges of water sent huge waves through the village. The flow picked up cars from the tourist car park at the top end of the village and carried them downstream. These mixed with tree trunks and branches from the wooded valley upstream, and damaged and knocked down buildings as they were swept down into the harbour and out to sea.

In all, 115 cars were lost. Water flowed into more than 100 homes and businesses, and four buildings were washed away completely. The village's infrastructure, including the water supply, sewers, power lines, telecommunications and roads, was badly damaged.

The rescue

The sudden rise of water trapped dozens of people. Tourists rescued some people from their cars. The emergency services called in helicopter crews who plucked people from roofs and trees. At the collapsing tourist information centre, 12 people were lifted from the roof. Rescuers feared that the water had swept people out to sea. Boats and helicopters scanned 32 kilometres of coastline, and divers searched the harbour. It turned out that, miraculously, nobody had been killed.

EYEWITNESS

❝ Cars started to move and I watched the water rising. In less than a minute it was up to the bottom of the car doors. I heard people screaming and realized that they were trapped in their cars, unable to get out because of the force of the water against the doors. People were calling out of their sunroofs for help, some frozen by fear and unwilling to get out of their cars; they had to be physically dragged out. ❞

Rachelle Strauss, tourist, Boscastle

Rebuilding Boscastle

The Boscastle flood was distressing for the residents and tourists, who watched as their homes, businesses and cars were wrecked by the water. It was the middle of the summer holidays and the tourist attractions, souvenir shops, hotels and guest houses lost all their custom. But the residents, the authorities and volunteers worked hard to recover from the disaster. They began by removing the tonnes of silt and other debris from the streets and buildings, and salvaging any belongings they could. Some buildings were structurally dangerous and had to be supported before the damage inside could be assessed.

Over the following months, the buildings were repaired and rebuilt and the infrastructure was restored. By spring 2005, nearly all of Boscastle's tourist facilities had reopened, just in time for the new tourist season. On 1 May 2005, less than a year after the devastating flood, residents celebrated the regeneration of Boscastle village.

PREVIOUS FLOODS

Boscastle has been flooded fairly regularly for hundreds of years, although the 2004 flood is the worst on record. Flash floods hit the village in 1827, 1950 and 1958. The 1958 flood started in just 20 minutes, killing one resident who was washed off his feet.

Many homes in Boscastle were left full of stinking mud carried in by the flood. Clearing up was a lengthy and depressing process.

FLOOD COSTS

- No deaths
- 60 buildings flooded
- 4 buildings completely destroyed
- Road bridge parapets destroyed
- 300 metres of sewers blocked and damaged
- 115 cars destroyed

Flood reports

In the UK, the Environment Agency is responsible for building and operating flood defences, and for monitoring river levels and issuing flood warnings. In 1996, eight years before the Boscastle flood, it carried out a study of the flood risks on the Valency River. The study concluded that Boscastle's storm drains should be improved, and plans were made to do this. The work was due to start in September 2004, a month after the disaster, but it is unlikely that the improvements would have made any difference because of the severity of the flood.

Another study was made after the flood. Experts analyzed information about the storms, the rainfall and the geography of the area. They concluded that the flood of 2004 was a 400-year flood, meaning that there is only a 1 in 400 chance of such a flood happening during any year. Because the risk of such a severe flood happening again is so low, the local authorities allowed people to rebuild the buildings destroyed by the flood where they originally stood.

Reducing the risk

Efforts are being made to reduce the damage that future floods might cause in Boscastle. The Valency River has been cleared of debris that could block storm drains. A new culvert (covered drain) has been built to carry flood water from the Jordan River through the village. The authorities are also considering options such as widening the river channel and building overflow culverts and flood walls.

NEW ORLEANS, USA, 2005

The city of New Orleans is on the Gulf Coast of the USA. Hurricanes that sweep in from the Atlantic Ocean hit this coast regularly, bringing storm surges and huge waves. On 29 August 2005, New Orleans and other towns on the Gulf Coast were flooded by the storm surge of Hurricane Katrina. Although plenty of warning was given, more than 1,000 people died in New Orleans alone. This led to an investigation into why rescue efforts had failed so badly.

WIDESPREAD DAMAGE

The storm surge also flooded other parts of the coastline to the east of New Orleans. Coastal cities such as Biloxi and Gulfport were badly damaged. In all, more than 1,800 people died in the floods caused by Hurricane Katrina.

New Orleans is crisscrossed by a network of rivers and canals, making the city highly vulnerable to floods in stormy weather.

Low-lying landscape

The USA's Gulf Coast is the edge of a wide coastal strip. It is only a few metres above sea level, with many islands and river deltas. The largest of the river deltas is the Mississippi delta, which is formed from sediment carried down the Mississippi River. Most of the Mississippi delta is marshy land. New Orleans is not on the coast, but it is almost entirely surrounded by water. Immediately to the north is Lake Pontchartrain, a lake that is actually a large inlet from the sea. The Mississippi runs through the southern part of New Orleans, and canals run into the city from the lake and the river. Many parts of New Orleans are below sea level. The water is held back by a system of levees.

Katrina approaches

Hurricane Katrina began as a tropical depression (an area of low air pressure) near the Bahamas. The storm developed into a hurricane and moved across the tip of Florida and into the Gulf of Mexico. It hit the Gulf Coast to the east of New Orleans. Its low pressure and winds of up to 204 kph produced a fearsome storm surge, up to 8.8 metres high, that raced towards the city.

Striking the city

Weather forecasters tracked the path and strength of Hurricane Katrina and quickly issued warnings for people on the Gulf Coast. As the storm approached New Orleans, the authorities advised people to evacuate the city. Hundreds of thousands left, but tens of thousands of poor people had no transport of their own and were stranded because buses
and trains had stopped running. By now the storm surge had already broken through some levees and was flowing over others. Water was pouring into the low-lying areas of the city.

EYEWITNESS

❝ I returned to New Orleans the first week of October to find my apartment totally destroyed. It had also been looted. I asked a police officer what I should do to protect myself and he told me to arm myself and not be afraid to shoot someone. The house I grew up in, in the Lower Ninth Ward area, was also completely destroyed. My 85-year-old uncle, who also lived in the area, just fell to his knees and cried when he saw what had happened to his house. ❞

Darryl Barthe, New Orleans resident

Trapped by the water

As the level of flood water rose, tens of thousands of people were trapped in their homes, offices and in other buildings. Some climbed into attics, but were caught by the rising water and drowned. The water mixed with oil, gasoline, dead animals, mud and other debris, forming a stinking soup in the streets. Water supplies, sanitation and power were lost. People took refuge on the city's bridges. Many were directed to the Louisiana Superdome, a massive sports stadium, and to the nearby New Orleans Convention Centre, which were both official hurricane shelters. Hundreds of patients, doctors and nurses were trapped in the city's hospitals.

Residents of New Orleans, trapped on the roof of their home, wait to be rescued by helicopter.

A delayed rescue

The people stranded in New Orleans, and people watching the disaster on television around the world, expected that flood victims would be rescued within a few hours, taken to shelters and given emergency supplies of food and water. Some people were lifted from rooftops by US Coast Guard helicopters. Others were rescued by friends and neighbours. However, four days passed before the US National Guard entered the city. In the meantime, there were only local police and firefighters to help people. They did their best, but the scale of the problem was too large for them to manage, and many were attacked by criminal gangs. Until fleets of buses came to take them to safety, people had to break into shops to find bottled water and food, and they had no toilets.

SLOW RECOVERY

It took a year to repair the levees and pump all the flood water out of the city. Slowly, the city is recovering. But at the beginning of 2007, many districts were still in ruins and may never be rebuilt. Tens of thousands of residents who moved to neighbouring cities have stayed. They are unlikely ever to return to New Orleans because they fear a repeat of the disaster.

Who to blame?

Even before the survivors had finally been evacuated, people began to ask why the residents of New Orleans had been left to fend for themselves. A government report published in 2006 blamed the local and national governments for failing to be prepared for such a disaster, for failing to keep the levees in good repair, and for failing to communicate with each other to organize a rescue.

Filthy flood water had to be pumped out of the city through huge pipes.

Flood prediction and defence

The threat from floods is reduced by accurate flood prediction. Flood warnings given in good time allow people to evacuate safely, to activate flood protection plans and to build temporary flood defences. Flood defences prevent flooding from happening, and reduce the severity of floods.

Weather forecasting

Accurate weather forecasts allow agencies that monitor river levels to predict floods. Hydrologists take previous rainfall and flood patterns into account and use computer models to help their predictions. They also take data from rain gauges and river-level gauging stations to track the progress of floods. Flash floods are harder to predict than river floods because the rainfall that causes them is often sudden and localized. Weather forecasters also track the storms that cause coastal flooding. They try to predict the height of storm surges and where the storm will hit coasts.

Flood warnings

Agencies work out the areas most likely to be flooded by a river, and give out flood warnings on the radio, television and websites. They have flood maps that show them which areas are at risk when the flood waters are at various depths.

WATCH AND WARN

Countries including the USA and the UK issue a Flood Watch if flooding is possible, and a Flood Warning if severe flooding is imminent.

The Thames Flood Barrier closes during very high tides to protect London from flooding.

Flood defences

The structures built to prevent rivers from flooding are embankments (also called levees or dykes), flood walls, dams, diversion channels and storage pools. Embankments raise the level of river banks, stopping the water from overflowing. Dams store flood water until it is safe to release it. Diversion channels and storage pools remove water from a river to lower its level. Coastal defences include dykes and barrages, which have gates that close to stop storm surges from moving up rivers.

Dams such as this one in China can catch or release water to control river levels in times of heavy rain.

Future floods

There is not much doubt that global warming is changing the Earth's climates. These changes will alter the pattern of floods. More intense storms will bring extra flooding to some places. Other places may see less flooding. Sea-level rises caused by global warming will increase the risk of coastal floods from high tides and storm surges.

No matter how well we can predict the rain and storms that lead to floods, and no matter how many flood defences we build, flooding will continue to be a threat in the future.

AGAINST FLOOD PROTECTION

Some hydrologists think that flood defences actually make the risk of severe floods worse. Defences such as dams and embankments hold back flood water, but if they fail the flooding can be far worse than it would have been if the defences had not been built.

Glossary

air pressure The push that air makes on everything in the Earth's atmosphere. Also called atmospheric pressure.

atmosphere The layer of air surrounding Earth.

caisson A huge concrete or steel container that is dropped into a river and filled with concrete, making it extremely heavy.

cholera A potentially fatal disease, carried in contaminated water. Symptoms include severe diarrhoea, cramps and vomiting.

culvert A pipe (made of plastic, steel or concrete) that carries water under a road.

cyclone An area of low pressure that winds circle around, creating a violent storm.

dam A solid barrier, like a wall, built across a valley to hold back the water in a river.

debris Scattered material, such as tree branches or building rubble, that has been dislodged or broken and left behind after a flood or other disaster.

dyke An embankment, normally made of earth, that protects low land from flooding.

dysentery An infectious disease that causes severe diarrhoea.

estuary The wide, lowest part of a river, where river water mixes with salt water as the river meets the sea.

evacuate To move away from a dangerous place to somewhere safe.

floodplain A wide, flat area of land alongside a river, which becomes covered with water when the river floods.

global warming The gradual warming of the Earth's atmosphere, thought to be caused mainly by the burning of oil, coal and gas.

gravity The force that pulls everything towards the Earth or the Sun or Moon.

hydrologist A scientist who studies the movement of water in rivers, through rocks, and so on.

infrastructure Things built for services and communications, such as roads, telephone cables, electricity pylons and water pipes.

irrigate To supply water to farmland along channels and pipes.

LEDC A less economically developed country (one where average income for people is very low and industry is sparse).

levee An embankment along the side of a river, either natural or artificial.

MEDC A more economically developed country (one where average income for people is high and industry is plentiful).

mineral A chemical, found in rocks, that is important to plant and crop growth.

monsoon A wind that blows across Asia at certain times of year, bringing heavy rains.

peninsula A long, narrow area of land that sticks out into the sea.

polder An area of land reclaimed from the sea. It is normally below sea level.

sanitation The collection and treatment of waste water.

satellite A scientific object that revolves in space, usually carrying equipment that can transmit signals to and from Earth.

sediment Particles of rock or soil carried along by the water in a river.

seismic Relates to earth movements and all aspects of the study of earthquakes.

source The place where a river starts, such as a lake or a spring.

storm surge A rise in sea level under a storm, caused by low air pressure and high winds.

tsunami A series of waves at sea, caused by an undersea earthquake, landslide or volcanic explosion.

tributary A river flowing into a larger river.

water vapour The gas form of water, produced when water is heated.

Further Information

Books

Nature's Fury: Flood!
Anita Ganeri
Franklin Watts, 2006

Floods
Michael Allaby
Facts on File, 2003

Wild Water: Floods
Tony Allan
Raintree, 2005

Natural Disasters (Eyewitness Guides)
Claire Watts
Dorling Kindersley, 2006

Websites

www.environment-agency.gov.uk/ subjects/flood The floods section of the UK's Environment Agency.

www.fema.gov/kids/floods.htm Children's webpage from the US Federal Emergency Management Agency (FEMA).

www.deltawerken.com Site of the Delta Works, the coastal flood protection scheme of the Netherlands.

www.geoprojects.co.uk/Keyfile/ KeyBoscastle.htm Information about the Boscastle flash flood, including photographs of the damage caused.

Index

Natural Disasters

Contents of titles in the series: